Y0-BVR-278

CABIN IN THE SNOW

✳ Book Two ✳ of the Prairie Skies Series

DEBORAH HOPKINSON

✳

Illustrated by PATRICK FARICY

ALADDIN PAPERBACKS

New York   London   Toronto   Sydney   Singapore

First Aladdin Paperbacks edition September 2002

Text copyright © 2002 by Deborah Hopkinson
Illustrations copyright © 2002 by Patrick Faricy

A Ready-for-Chapters Book

ALADDIN PAPERBACKS
An imprint of Simon & Schuster
Children's Publishing Division
1230 Avenue of the Americas
New York, NY 10020

Designed by Debra Sfetsios
The text of this book was set in ITC Century Book.
Printed in the United States of America
4 6 8 10 9 7 5
Library of Congress Control Number 2002102033
ISBN-13: 978-0-689-84351-8 (ISBN-10: 0-689-84351-8)

THE KANSAS EMIGRANTS

(To the tune of "Auld Lang Syne")

We cross the prairie, as of old

Our fathers crossed the sea;

To make the West as they the East

The Homestead of the Free.

—John Greenleaf Whittier

ACKNOWLEDGMENTS

Special thanks to Kansas historian Paul K. Stuewe for helpful suggestions; to Deborah Wiles for her careful reading of the story; to Michele Hill for tramping through the prairie grass with me; and to the helpful librarians of the Kansas State Historical Society.

I would also like to thank the Southwest Parks and Memorial Association for permission to reprint the recipe for Apple Fruit Cake from *An Army Wife's Cookbook with Household Hints and Home Remedies,* compiled and edited by Mary L. Williams, published by the Southwest Parks and Memorial Association (Tucson: 1972).

For Judy, Tom, Matt, and Mason

✳

CHAPTER
ONE

"Charlie. Charlie Keller. What *are* you doing? Papa's waiting!"

Charlie looked up. His sister was racing toward him, her hair flying. She looked small against the wide, empty sky.

"I'm coming, Ida Jane!" Charlie ran to meet her. But the wind snatched his words away. *The wind in Kansas never stops*, he thought.

Charlie held out a strand of grass for Ida Jane to see. "I was picking prairie grass to send home to Grandpa."

Charlie took out his letter, slipped the grass into it, and put it carefully in his pocket.

"If you want to mail that today, you'd better come. Papa's ready to go to town *now*." Ida Jane pulled at his sleeve.

1

"Wait. I've got to call Lion." Charlie stopped. "I can't leave without him."

Charlie tried to whistle, but the wind tore at his lips. He cupped his hands and hollered, "Lion. Lion!"

Deep in the tall grass, a golden brown dog lifted his head. He barked once, then bounded toward them, his mouth open.

"Lion looks like he's smiling," said Charlie, laughing.

But Ida Jane hopped from one foot to the other and frowned. "You need to train Lion to stay close, Charlie. He could wander off in Lawrence and get lost."

"I'll watch him," Charlie promised. Charlie didn't want to lose his young dog. Finding Lion was the best thing that had happened to him since moving to Kansas last spring.

"Now, Charlie, make sure you and Papa get *all* the supplies on Momma's list," Ida Jane ordered. "Momma's afraid Papa will spend so much time talking to the other free-soil settlers he'll forget the cornmeal!"

"Papa does like to catch up on the news," said Charlie. "He cares so much about making Kansas a free state, sometimes that's all he can think about."

Ida Jane sighed. "I know. It's just that . . . I don't want Momma to get upset. Things are hard for her right now."

Charlie fell silent. With a new baby on the way, Momma moved more slowly these days. Not only that, but she had seemed extra quiet lately. Sad even. Charlie couldn't remember the last time he'd heard her sing.

Lion ran up and barked twice. His tongue lolled out, and he smiled his happy dog smile. Then he raced ahead toward their small cabin.

Ida Jane pulled her shawl close. "When the baby comes, you'll have to help more. You're nine now, Charlie. You have to pay attention. You can't spend all your time dreaming and roaming the prairie with Lion. I don't know what you look at this time of year anyway," she added. "It's not like you can collect bugs and flowers now. Everything is brown and dead."

It didn't look brown and dead to Charlie, though. Especially not when the prairie grass sparkled like dark gold in the frosty morning sun.

"I'm getting used to Kansas," Charlie had written in his letter to Grandpa. "I still miss you and old Danny and everything about Massachusetts. But I'm glad I have Lion. And just like you said, Grandpa, these prairie skies are big. So big I sometimes feel I could leap into the air and glide like a red-tailed hawk."

They were almost to the cabin when Charlie grabbed

3

Ida Jane's sleeve. "Ida Jane, is—is Momma going to be all right?"

Even though Ida Jane was only eleven, she usually had an answer for everything. This time, though, she didn't seem to know what to say. Instead she grabbed Charlie's hand and gave it a quick squeeze.

"I hope she'll be all right, Charlie," said Ida Jane. "I hope so with all my heart."

CHAPTER

TWO

Papa had hitched the oxen to the wagon. Momma and Sadie came out of the cabin to wave good-bye.

Sadie held her arms up to get a hug. "Bring me a peppermint stick, Pa!"

Papa smiled. "Only if you promise to mind your momma and not wander off, Sadie. Remember, you don't have a good nose like Lion does."

Sadie giggled. "That's because I'm not a dog, Papa."

Charlie said good-bye to Ida Jane, then patted his little sister on the head. "Good puppy, Sadie Sunshine," he teased.

Momma hugged him. "Now pay attention and help your papa, Charlie," she whispered.

Charlie felt his face go red. Momma was reminding him to pay attention too. Maybe Ida Jane was right. Maybe he *did* spend too much time dreaming.

It wasn't that Charlie didn't want to help. But sometimes he wished he were more like Ida Jane. She always seemed to know exactly what needed to be done—and how to do it. Ida Jane was good at helping Momma with cooking and sewing, and she could work outside with Papa in the fields too.

But whenever Charlie started a chore, like gathering firewood down at the creek, something always got his attention. Maybe it was a prairie wildflower he'd never seen before. Or a flash of red. Then he'd just have to stop to get a closer look at a red-winged blackbird.

Charlie climbed onto the wagon seat next to Papa. Lion scampered up beside him. Charlie patted his pocket. Grandpa's letter was safe.

Momma put her hand on Papa's arm. "Please be careful, James. I can't help worrying about trouble with the border ruffians."

"Don't fret, Sarah. It's been quiet all summer. Charlie and I should be home tonight or tomorrow morning," Papa told her.

And then they were off. Charlie waved until the cabin seemed no larger than a tiny box on the lonely prairie.

Charlie liked riding in the wagon with Papa. So did Lion. Lion wagged his tail so hard Charlie felt as if he were being hit in the ribs by a stick.

As they bumped along, Charlie couldn't stop thinking about what Momma had said. "Who exactly *are* the border ruffians, Papa?"

"Well, Charlie, do you remember my talking about the Kansas-Nebraska Act?"

"I think so," said Charlie slowly. "Kansas is a territory now. But someday it will become a state. The Kansas-Nebraska Act says that the people of Kansas, not the government, will vote on whether it becomes a free state or a slave state."

"Yes. And that's why abolitionists like us, who are against slavery, have come here: to make Kansas free," Papa said. "We want to stop slavery from spreading west.

"But Missouri is a slave state. Many people there want Kansas to be a slave state too," Papa added. "Some of these proslavery folks have settled in Kansas. Others—we call them border ruffians—still live in Missouri. But they'll do just about anything to make Kansas a slave state. They even stole our territorial election last March!"

"How did they do that, Papa?"

"They came from Missouri and voted for proslavery candidates for our legislature," said Papa, clenching his fist. "And then this bogus legislature appointed

Samuel Jones, a proslavery man who lives in Missouri, as *our* sheriff!"

Papa sighed. "Sometimes I fear Kansas Territory is just a box of tinder, waiting to burst into flames. It will only take one spark."

The town of Lawrence was bustling with wagons, horses, and people.

Papa pointed to one wagon being unloaded in front of a store. "We may not agree with our neighbors in Missouri. But we depend on goods from Missouri just the same."

They passed a tailor's shop and a store that sold tubs, pails, and brooms. Suddenly Papa stopped the wagon.

"Would you look at that, Charlie!" he exclaimed. "Let's find out how much that wooden rocker costs."

A rocking chair for Momma! With the baby coming, it would be the perfect gift. They didn't have one comfortable chair in their tiny cabin.

A rocking chair might make Momma sing again, Charlie thought.

The furniture shop was empty except for a stern-looking man with a long face, sipping coffee from a tin cup.

"Afternoon, folks," he said. "I'm Ed Dillon. Most folks call me Wooden Ed."

He winked at Charlie.

Charlie had to ask. "Why do they call you that, sir?"

"Don't rightly know. Might be on account of I like to make things out of wood," said Ed. He rubbed his face. "Or maybe it's got something to do with this long, serious mug of mine."

Papa grinned and stuck out his hand. "I'm James Keller. This is my son, Charlie. We've got a claim southwest of town, at Spring Creek. How much are your chairs?"

"Regular chairs are a dollar."

"How about the rocking chair?" Charlie asked.

"Well, Charlie, that rocker is another matter," said Wooden Ed. "Why, a nice painted wooden rocker like that is gonna cost you two dollars and seventy-five cents."

"Nearly three dollars!" cried Papa.

"Yup, and I can't take a penny less," said Ed, looking more serious than ever. "Wood is scarce in these parts, you know. Why, half the cabins in town have still got prairie hay or old carpet for floors. Folks are in for a cold, rough winter."

Charlie looked at Papa hopefully, but Papa shook his

head. The chair was too expensive. Wooden Ed was right. It would be a hard winter. They would need all their extra money for food.

"By the way, Mr. Keller," said Ed as they were leaving, "have you heard about the shooting?"

Papa froze. "Shooting? What shooting?"

"It happened a few days ago at Hickory Point, south of the Wakarusa River, about ten miles away," Ed told them. "A free-state man named Charles Dow was shot by Franklin Coleman, a proslavery man. Dow didn't even have a gun."

"That's an outrage!" exclaimed Papa.

Wooden Ed nodded. "Coleman has fled to Missouri, where his proslavery friends will protect him. But I hear Jacob Branson, who shared a cabin with Charles Dow, is fightin' mad about the death of his friend."

"What's going to happen now?" Papa asked.

Ed finished his coffee and shrugged. "Who can say? It don't look good."

Charlie wondered if this might be the spark Papa had been talking about, the spark that would cause a lot of trouble in Kansas.

CHAPTER
THREE

"Lion. Here, boy!"

Charlie stood outside Ed Dillon's store and looked left, then right. No Lion.

"Charlie, you need to pay more attention to training Lion," Papa scolded. "You told him to stay. But he's just like Sadie. He wanders off at the drop of a hat."

Charlie said quickly, "I'll find him, Papa. And I can still help you get the supplies."

"All right." Papa gave Charlie a dollar. "Buy a bushel of apples. Check at the little store at the end of the street. They had them last time I was here. Momma said she'd bake an apple pie if we got some."

Charlie trudged up and down the muddy roads, looking for Lion. Where could he be? Charlie felt his pocket.

He still hadn't mailed his letter to Grandpa, and he was supposed to be helping Papa get supplies. Instead he was looking for Lion.

Charlie had walked down just about every muddy path in town when he suddenly heard a yell. "Shoo. Shoo, away! Away from my chickens!"

Charlie ran. A woman stood outside a small cabin, holding a broom over her head. She was about to bring it down on Lion's head.

"Wait! Don't hit him. He won't hurt your chickens; he protects them. Lion, come here!"

Lion spotted Charlie and trotted over.

The woman shook her broom at Charlie. "You should watch your dog if you don't want him shot."

Charlie knelt down. Lion licked his face and whined happily.

"Please be good," Charlie begged. "You're going to get us both into trouble. Now let's run and find Papa."

Papa was loading a sack of cornmeal onto the wagon. He looked up. "I bought squashes for a penny a pound and a hundred pumpkins for one dollar and fifty cents. Did you get apples?"

Charlie opened his mouth, but no sound came out. He had been so excited to find Lion he had completely forgotten about the apples.

Without waiting for his answer, Papa continued. "Well, no matter. We'd better head home now. Besides, we still have dried apples left. I like the cake Momma makes with dried apples almost as well as her fresh apple pie."

Charlie swallowed and gave Papa back the dollar. He was afraid to tell Papa he hadn't even looked. Now, because of him, they wouldn't have real apple pie.

The sky faded from gray to black. By the time they headed for home, the short November day was nearly gone.

Lion snuggled next to Charlie on the wagon seat. Far off a wolf howled. Lion pricked up his ears and shivered.

Charlie tried to stay awake, but the bumping of the wagon made him sleepy. He felt his eyes get heavy. Next thing he knew he heard a shout.

"Who goes there?"

Charlie's eyes snapped open. It was dark now. But he could make out a group of men just ahead.

16

Papa answered the call. "I'm James Keller, a free-soil man from Spring Creek."

"Well, whaddya know?" one of the men answered. "You're just in time, James. Come join us."

It was Ed Dillon, the man from the store. Behind him stood about a dozen men. Some carried rifles. In the cold night their breaths came in white puffs.

Charlie grabbed hold of Lion. Why were these men out on the road so late?

"What's going on, Ed?" Papa asked.

Ed spoke in a low voice. "Sheriff Samuel Jones has arrested Jacob Branson, the friend of the man who was killed. The sheriff claims Branson is dangerous."

"That's ridiculous! Branson hasn't done anything. Sheriff Jones can't go around arresting people for no reason," exclaimed Papa.

"Well, he has. And we don't like it. We have some good men here." Ed nodded toward his friends. "We aim to rescue Branson—before he gets hurt."

Another man stepped forward. "We think Sheriff Jones and his men will be heading this way soon. Are you with us, Keller?"

Lion whined. Charlie held him close. It would be just like Lion to jump off the wagon and get in the way.

Charlie felt Papa stiffen.

"Jones *was* appointed sheriff, even though we think that was wrong," Papa said slowly, picking his words carefully. "If we rescue Branson, we'll be breaking the law of Kansas Territory."

Ed Dillon scoffed. "Law? What kind of law arrests a man for no reason?"

Another man nodded and said, "Ed's right. We have to act now. If we don't rescue Branson, Jones and his border ruffian friends might kill him."

Papa nodded slowly. Papa wanted to help, Charlie realized. After all, this was why they'd come to Kansas: to stand up for the free-state cause.

"I'll stay in the wagon, out of the way," Charlie offered.

"Don't worry about your boy. He'll be safe, tucked away in the bushes. We'll simply ask Jones to turn Branson over to us," Ed told Papa. "We don't aim to fight."

Papa put his hand on Charlie's arm. "You brave enough for this, son?"

Charlie gulped. "Yes, Papa. Besides, I'll have Lion right beside me."

"Whatever you do, stay out of sight," Papa ordered.

Charlie curled up in the back of the wagon next to the sack of cornmeal. He shivered and rested his cheek against Lion's warm body. "It's cold, Lion."

A long time went by, and nothing happened. Charlie wiggled his toes to keep them warm. Suddenly Lion began to growl, soft and low.

"Shh . . . ," Charlie warned.

At first Charlie didn't hear anything.

Clomp, clomp, clomp. Horses! Coming closer!

Charlie heard Ed Dillon say, "It's them all right."

CHAPTER
FOUR

Charlie peered over the edge of the wagon. In the pale moonlight he could see the riders coming closer.

"Looks like a lot of them," he whispered to Lion.

As Charlie watched, Papa and the other free-soil men formed a line, blocking the road. The men on horseback pulled up sharply. Their horses snorted and whinnied.

"What's going on here?" hollered a rider.

"We're friends of Jacob Branson. Is he there with you?" Ed Dillon called.

"Yes, I'm here," Charlie heard someone say. "I'm a prisoner."

"Come over here with us, Jacob," a free-state man said.

Charlie counted about fifteen proslavery men. Their rifles glinted in the moonlight. Would these men let Jacob Branson go without a fight?

One of the riders barked a warning. "If you move, Branson, we'll shoot you."

Charlie saw the proslavery men raise their rifles. The free-state men lifted theirs too.

"Don't be foolish. If you shoot, not a man of you will leave alive," said one of the men on Papa's side. "Come on, Branson."

Slowly a large man with a straw hat crossed over to the free-state side, riding a mule.

"Is that your mule?" someone asked him.

Jacob Branson shook his head. "No, it's theirs."

"Well, get off and let it go."

Branson got off the mule and gave it a slap on its rump.

Charlie watched closely. What would happen now?

"Now listen here. I'm Samuel Jones, the sheriff of Douglas County," said a tall man on a horse. "Branson is my prisoner. I have a warrant for his arrest."

Charlie could hear the anger in Papa's voice. "Samuel Jones? We've heard of a postmaster in Westport, Missouri, by that name. But we don't know any *real* sheriff named Jones!"

Charlie held his breath and dug his nails into his palms. *Oh, please let Papa be safe*, he thought.

Suddenly a proslavery man moved. At first Charlie thought something bad would happen. But the man lowered his gun. "I ain't going to shoot," he said.

For a long moment no one moved. Then, slowly, the other men lowered their guns too. Charlie let out his breath.

The men argued some more. Then Sheriff Jones and his men turned around and rode away—without Jacob Branson.

"The free-state men have won!" Charlie whispered to Lion.

But Lion was sound asleep, snoring softly.

As soon as the Missouri men had gone, Jacob Branson thanked his free-state friends for rescuing him. Papa and the other men cheered.

Ed Dillon held up his hand. "It's good that Jacob is safe now. But I have a feeling our troubles aren't over."

"I agree," Papa said. "Sheriff Jones might try to get back at us. He knows Lawrence is a free-soil town. He might decide to use this an excuse to attack it."

"That's right," Ed Dillon agreed. "We all know Sheriff Jones and his border ruffian friends want to make us leave Kansas."

"So what do we do?" several voices asked at once.

"We'd better get back to Lawrence. We've got to warn the town," said Ed Dillon. He looked over and spotted Charlie. "Are you with us free-soilers, young feller?"

"Yes, sir," cried Charlie.

On the way back to Lawrence, Charlie shivered and beat his arms to stay warm. Once he felt something swoop down low close to his head. He jumped, then realized it was just a big owl, with silent, velvety wings.

Charlie wondered what would happen next. Would there be a battle between the proslavery men and the free-soilers?

And what about Momma, Ida Jane, and Sadie? Would they be safe at Spring Creek?

CHAPTER
FIVE

Charlie dreamed it was raining. But when he opened his eyes, he started to laugh. Lion was licking his face.

"Lion, you're getting me all wet," he cried. Lion pushed his head against Charlie's hand and barked. Lion was ready for breakfast.

Charlie sat up. He was still in the back of the wagon, covered with a blanket.

"It's morning, and we're back in Lawrence, Lion," he said, trying to remember when he'd finally fallen asleep.

The wagon stood in front of the Free State Hotel. The steps to the building weren't finished, so Charlie walked up a wooden plank to go look for Papa. Sure enough, Papa was in the long dining room drinking coffee with Ed Dillon and the other free-soil men.

Papa called, "There you are! Come and have some breakfast, Charlie. I didn't want to wake you."

Charlie sat between Papa and Ed Dillon. Ed leaned close and grinned at Charlie. "That was some excitement last night, wasn't it, young feller?"

"What's going to happen now?" Charlie asked.

Ed stopped smiling. He said, "Well, I wouldn't be surprised if Jones is gathering men from Missouri and the proslavery town of Franklin right now."

Franklin! Charlie knew that town. That was where Flory Morgan and her father lived. Charlie and Flory had met on the steamboat to Kansas City. Flory and her father were from Missouri. Charlie frowned. Did this mean Mr. Morgan might fight against Papa?

"Kansas is going to need strong hearts right now, to battle for what is right," said Ed, looking at Papa.

Papa nodded slowly. "Charlie, we became pioneers in Kansas to help the free-state cause. I can't leave right now. I must stay in Lawrence, at least for a few days. But—"

Charlie swallowed hard. Suddenly he realized what Papa needed him to do.

"The team knows the way home," Papa went on. "I fed and watered them while you were sleeping. But you can't be running off after Lion or stopping to look at birds. Can I depend on you, son?"

Charlie looked down at his hands. In his heart he wasn't sure. But he knew he had to try.

"I can do it, Papa. I can drive the team home."

Charlie brought Lion leftover corn biscuits for breakfast.

"Follow the road south to Spring Creek," Papa told him. "If you meet anyone, tell them you're fetching supplies for your mother."

Papa handed Charlie a note. "Give this to Momma. It explains everything. I should be home in a few days. You'll be safe at Spring Creek. If Sheriff Jones and his men do come, they'll head straight for Lawrence."

As Charlie went to put Papa's note in his pocket, he felt something there. "My letter to Grandpa! I forgot to mail it."

"I'll post it. And maybe we'll have a letter from home." Papa patted Charlie's arm. "You'd better head out. Go as quickly as you can. Momma will be worried."

Charlie climbed up onto the wagon. He was setting out for home. Alone.

But I'm not really alone. I have Lion, he reminded himself.

We can do this together, he thought. *I know we can.*

CHAPTER
SIX

"Five. That's five red-tailed hawks we've seen," Charlie told Lion. "I like how they hang in the sky. The hunting is good for hawks here."

Lion wagged his tail and sniffed the air. He barked once.

"I think it's all right if we look at hawks once in a while," Charlie added. "Just as long as we watch the road. And just as long as *you* don't run off!"

Lion nuzzled Charlie's arm. So far so good.

"We're going to show everyone they're wrong about us, Lion," Charlie told his dog. "I'm going to pay attention. And you're not going to wander away."

But no sooner had Charlie said the words than he saw something move in the grass ahead. A rabbit!

Lion saw it too. He whined, wrinkling his forehead. His whole body shook. His fur stood on end.

In a flash the rabbit disappeared into the grass. Lion leaped off the wagon after it.

"Oh no! Lion, come back," Charlie pleaded.

But Lion didn't stop. He vanished into the grass.

"Lion, get back here. Lion!" Charlie yelled. But all he could see was the grass rippling in the wind.

"You have to come back, Lion. I can't wait for you," Charlie shouted, desperate now. "I can't leave the wagon."

The prairie had never seemed so empty. Charlie tried not to cry. More than anything he wanted to leave the wagon on the road and find his dog.

"But I have to get the supplies home to Momma," he said aloud. "That's the most important thing, no matter what."

Up ahead Charlie made out some specks in the road. As he watched, the specks grew larger.

Charlie gripped the reins tighter. He could see two men on horseback now, one ahead of the other. *What if they're border ruffians?* thought Charlie. He glanced at the back of the wagon. Potatoes, cornmeal, molasses. Precious food that his family needed.

It would be easy for these men to steal everything he had, even the wagon.

He couldn't let that happen. But he had no idea how to stop it.

"Hey, boy, what you got there?" said the lead rider. He stopped his horse in the middle of the road, blocking Charlie's way.

The man had pale greenish eyes and a red nose. He carried his reins in one hand and a rifle in the other. He came closer and glared at Charlie.

"You seem mighty young to be haulin' those valuable goods all by yourself," the man said. "Looks like you might need some help."

"I'm almost home. I—I don't need help," Charlie sputtered. If only Papa hadn't stayed behind in Lawrence. If only Lion were beside him to bark and growl.

Charlie took a breath. "I have a sick mother and two sisters."

"Is that so?" said the man. His green eyes looked mean.

Charlie's hands felt hot, though the wind was cold. His mind raced. What could he say? What could he do to get away from the man?

Just then the other man rode up. "What's going on?"

Charlie stared. Somehow this man looked familiar.

31

Suddenly he knew. It was Mr. Morgan, Flory's father.

The man with the green eyes pointed to the goods in the back of the wagon. "Looks like this is our lucky day."

Mr. Morgan frowned. "Wait a minute. I know this boy."

Green Eyes looked suspicious. "Are he and his folks free-soilers?"

Charlie held his breath. *Mr. Morgan knows Papa is against slavery,* he thought. He looked into Mr. Morgan's face. *Please don't give us away,* he pleaded silently.

Mr. Morgan said firmly, "This boy and his family are my friends."

Green Eyes shook his finger at Mr. Morgan. "Sheriff Jones won't like it if I let supplies slip through my fingers."

Sheriff Jones! Charlie caught his breath. Sheriff Jones probably needed supplies to feed the men he was gathering in Franklin, men who might attack Lawrence at any moment.

Mr. Morgan turned to Green Eyes. "I'm going to escort my young friend here a little ways down the road. I'll catch up with you."

Charlie shivered, partly from the cold, partly from fear. He looked from one man to the other.

Then Green Eyes raised his gun in the air.

CHAPTER
SEVEN

Mr. Morgan put up his hand. His voice was firm. "You ride on, like I said. I'll catch up with you."

Green Eyes asked, "Whose side are you on, Morgan?"

But after a moment he lowered his rifle. He spurred his horse and rode on.

Mr. Morgan looked at Charlie and smiled. "Last time we met your little sister had wandered away. Now you. Where's your pa?"

"He had to stay in Lawrence, because of the trouble. And I'm not wandering, Mr. Morgan, I'm going home," Charlie said. "But my dog, Lion, has run off. I'm afraid he's lost."

Mr. Morgan frowned. "He could be miles away by now."

Charlie looked out over the endless grass. Where was Lion?

"I can try one thing," Mr. Morgan offered.

He put two fingers to his lips and let out a whistle so loud and sharp Charlie had to cover his ears.

The wind blew gently over the surface of the grass. It reminded Charlie of a rolling, golden sea.

Charlie shook his head. "I guess he's gone . . . I don't think he heard—"

"Woof!"

Suddenly Lion's head appeared. He looked like a rabbit himself, bounding up and down so he could see above the high grass.

"There he is," cried Charlie. "Lion, come!"

Mr. Morgan laughed as Lion burst out of the grass. "Let's get the two of you home."

Momma's face was like a pale moon in the dark doorway of the cabin. She took everything in. The stranger. No Papa.

Her voice was soft and scared. She pulled her shawl around her. "Charlie, is everything all right? Where's your father? And who is this man?"

"Papa is fine. He had to stay in Lawrence," Charlie began.

Mr. Morgan stepped forward and tipped his hat. "Mrs. Keller, I'm Jake Morgan. You won't remember me. But

my daughter, Flory, and Charlie met on the steamboat last spring. We live in Franklin."

"I see." Momma frowned. She knew Franklin was a proslavery settlement.

Charlie spoke quickly. "I'm fine, Momma, really. Mr. Morgan just wanted to make sure I got home."

"I'm obliged to you, Mr. Morgan," Momma said, almost in a whisper. She leaned against the doorframe.

Momma is sick, Charlie realized.

"I'd best be going," said Mr. Morgan. He started to leave, then turned back to Momma. "Unless—unless there is anything I can do to help you, ma'am."

Momma drew her shawl closer. Her voice was sharp. "No. No, thank you, Mr. Morgan. We don't need help."

But looking at Momma's pale face, Charlie wasn't so sure.

CHAPTER
EIGHT

Charlie fed and watered the oxen as quickly as he could. When he stepped into the cabin, Sadie was huddled in the corner, staring with wide eyes. She jumped up and threw her arms around his waist. "I'm glad you're back, Charlie."

Ida Jane stood beside Momma's bed, a tin cup of water in her hand. Momma lay curled up, her eyes closed.

"Momma's sick," Sadie said, her voice trembling a little.

Momma opened her eyes. "Charlie, why didn't Papa come home? Tell me."

"Lawrence might be attacked, Momma. Papa had to stay and help defend the town." Charlie handed Momma the note. But she groaned and closed her eyes again.

"She's been feeling poorly since early morning," said Ida Jane softly. "I kept hoping you and Papa would come home."

All at once Charlie understood. The baby was coming—earlier than expected. Momma had been too afraid to tell Mr. Morgan. After all, he was a stranger. She wasn't sure she could trust him.

But Charlie knew Mr. Morgan would have helped. If only he hadn't ridden away. Charlie looked at Ida Jane. "What should we do now?"

"Can you run and fetch Mrs. Engle? The Engles live less than two miles away." Ida Jane straightened her shoulders. "I'll try to keep Momma comfortable."

"Do you know what to do if the baby comes?" Charlie asked quietly.

"I'll—I'll just . . . keep the room warm and—and—" Ida Jane took a deep breath. "Do what I have to."

She gave Charlie a push. "Now go!"

"One, two, one, two."

Charlie's feet pounded out a rhythm. He had to keep moving fast. But he was starting to feel tired. He hadn't slept much in the cold, cramped wagon.

Now he had to run. He had to get help for Momma.

Charlie came around a bend and spotted a rider on horseback coming toward him.

The rider waved. At first Charlie thought it might be Mr. Morgan. But it was their neighbor, Mrs. Engle.

Mrs. Engle pulled her horse up beside him.

"Momma needs help. . . ." Charlie gasped.

Mrs. Engle nodded. She had dark hair and a pleasant smile. "I know, Charlie. That nice Mr. Morgan stopped by to tell me he feared her time had come. Luckily we have a horse. But he would have given us his, I think."

"Oh! Where did Mr. Morgan go?" asked Charlie.

"He said he had to get back to his daughter. Now, Charlie, just turn around and come home," Mrs. Engle told him. "I'm going to ride ahead. I'm sure everything will be fine."

"Today is Thursday, November twenty-ninth," said Momma, sitting up in bed. "Back home in Massachusetts we celebrated a day of thanksgiving this time of year, but I don't expect people in these parts do that."

"We should celebrate anyway," said Charlie. "We can celebrate the good neighbors who helped us when we needed them."

"And we can celebrate Baby Henry," added Sadie, patting her new brother's soft head, as he lay cradled in Momma's arms. "Can you make an apple pie, Momma?"

"Sadie! You know better than that. Mrs. Engle said Momma should rest in bed for a few more days," scolded Ida Jane. "Besides, we don't have any apples left."

After helping deliver the baby, Mrs. Engle had stayed two nights before going home to her own family. Before she left, she told Ida Jane and Charlie that Momma would be fine.

"Back home we made all kinds of wonderful pies, didn't we?" Momma said softly. Her eyes filled with tears. "Cherry and pumpkin. And apple pie with apples from our own orchard."

More than ever Charlie wished he hadn't forgotten to buy fresh apples in town.

"Well, I can bake an apple cake with dried apples, Momma," offered Ida Jane. "Maybe Papa will even be home tonight to eat it."

Ida Jane set to work. Sadie and Charlie helped. Before long the cabin was filled with the rich smells of molasses, nutmeg, and cinnamon. But Papa did not appear.

Charlie wished he knew what was happening in Lawrence. Were the border ruffians about to attack the city? Would Papa be safe? Would he be coming home soon?

It was almost dark when Charlie heard a noise.

Knock, knock, knock!

CHAPTER
NINE

"Papa!" yelled Sadie.

But Charlie knew it wasn't Papa. Papa wouldn't knock. Charlie looked at Momma and Ida Jane.

Momma nodded. "Open it, Charlie. If border ruffians have come to steal from us, we won't be able to stop them."

When Charlie opened the door, he found himself staring into a pair of bright blue eyes the exact same color as a robin's egg.

"Hello, Massachusetts Charlie!" Flory Morgan smiled and held out a large basket. "Daddy and I brought you presents: butter, eggs, apples, and jam I made myself. Can you believe I made jam? Well, I did!"

Mr. Morgan tipped his hat and spoke to Momma. "Mrs. Keller, would it be all right if Flory and I come in?"

* * *

Ida Jane bristled when Momma asked her to make some tea for Mr. Morgan and Flory. Ida Jane remembered Flory from the steamboat. She didn't like the idea of having someone from Missouri in their house.

But Momma smiled and said, "Mr. Morgan, I want to thank you for letting my neighbor know I needed help. And I'm grateful to you for getting Charlie home safely."

Sadie piped up. "Flory and her papa helped me too when I got lost in the big city."

Momma frowned. "Whatever is Sadie talking about, Ida Jane?"

Ida Jane and Charlie looked sheepish.

"Momma, do you remember when we were in Kansas City last spring and Papa fell ill? Well, Sadie wandered off when you were busy nursing Papa," Ida Jane explained. "Flory and Mr. Morgan found her."

"Ida Jane, you were supposed to be watching Sadie that day," Momma scolded.

Ida Jane bit her lip and was silent. Charlie stared at the floor.

Mr. Morgan cleared his throat. "Mrs. Keller, I was glad to help. And please accept my congratulations.

But today I have come to ask *you* for a favor."

"What is it?" asked Momma.

"Hundreds of men are gathering in Franklin," said Mr. Morgan. "Sheriff Jones has called up many of his rough, hotheaded friends from Missouri. He plans to attack Lawrence."

So that's why Papa hasn't come home, Charlie realized. *The trouble isn't over.*

"I don't believe fighting is the way to settle differences. I hope I can convince my neighbors to stay calm, Mrs. Keller," Mr. Morgan went on. "But right now Franklin does not feel safe."

Momma clutched Baby Henry closer.

"Ma'am, my wife died of cholera last year." Mr. Morgan put his arm on Flory's shoulder. "My daughter is all I have in the world. I worry about her staying in Franklin. There are rumors that free-state men are threatening to burn homes and run people off. Your claim is out of the way here. I—I wonder if she might stay with you for a few days."

Before Charlie's mother could answer, Flory spoke up. "I won't be any trouble, ma'am. I may be skinny, but I'm strong. I can sew and clean. I'm the best cook for my age that I have ever met. I can sing songs to the baby oo. I know lots of tremendously wonderful songs."

Charlie held his breath, waiting.

Momma said slowly, "I know my husband would be as grateful to you as I am, Mr. Morgan. Flory may stay. It is the least we can do to repay your kindness."

Sadie was excited about having a guest. She followed Flory around like a puppy.

But Ida Jane sulked all during dinner. "Papa would never have let her stay," she growled in Charlie's ear.

Bedtime was worse. Ida Jane didn't like sharing her mattress of prairie hay with a girl from Missouri. "You can sleep on the outside, and Sadie will sleep next to you," Ida Jane told Flory.

The cabin was bitter cold at night. The wind lashed at the walls and seemed to whine endlessly. Charlie lay awake, listening. He felt lonely without Papa. Then Charlie heard Flory's strong, sweet voice.

> "Oh, Shenandoah, I long to hear you,
>
> Way hey, you rolling river!
>
> Oh, Shenandoah, I long to hear you.
>
> Away, we're bound away
>
> 'cross the wide Missouri."

It was such a pretty, peaceful song that Charlie couldn't help smiling.

But when Charlie opened his eyes in the morning, the peacefulness was gone. Ida Jane and Flory were standing nose to nose in the center of the cabin, hands on their hips.

"You shouldn't come into someone's house and act like a know-it-all," Ida Jane was saying. "Besides, my momma's just had a new baby. We haven't had a chance to go fetch more wood."

"Girls, please . . . ," said Momma.

Flory turned to Momma. "Begging your pardon, ma'am, but perhaps you haven't heard about the prairie blizzards out this way. My daddy says the snow will be up to here before long!" Flory raised her hands as high as her head.

She paused only long enough to take a breath. "When I got the fire going this morning, I noticed you surely could use more wood. Daddy says it's a good idea to pile up wood inside the cabin too, so it will be dry and close at hand in case of a storm."

Momma nodded weakly. "Perhaps you're right. We are so new to this hard life. My husband was a store-keeper back home. And I've been feeling so poorly. . . ."

"Why, Mrs. Keller, I think you are doing tremendously wonderful. Just look at your beautiful baby boy!" Flory rushed over and grabbed Momma's hand. "Please don't fret. Charlie and I will fetch enough wood to keep us warm. Why, it will feel almost as if we're lying on the banks of the Big Muddy on a hot summer day!"

"What's the Big Muddy, Flory?" Sadie wanted to know.

"Why, you know that, Sadie. It's the Missouri River, the river that brought you to Kansas," said Flory. "Remember, I sang you a beautiful song about it last night, called 'Shenandoah.' Listen:

"Oh, Shenandoah, I love your daughter,
Way hey, you rolling river!
Oh, Shenandoah, I love your daughter.
Away, we're bound away
'cross the wide Missouri.

"Missouri she's a mighty river,
Way hey, you rolling river!
When she rolls down, her topsails shiver.
Away, we're bound away
'cross the wide Missouri."

As she sang, Flory grabbed Sadie's hands and spun her around. Sadie giggled. Charlie caught Ida Jane tapping her toe. *Grandpa would like this song*, thought Charlie. He decided to ask Flory to write the words down for him.

Charlie looked over at Momma and smiled. For just a second Momma smiled back.

CHAPTER
TEN

"This sky puts me in mind of snow," said Flory about a week later, as they walked back to the cabin from feeding the animals. "It has an awful gray look to it."

Charlie nodded. "It's December now. The sky at home used to look like this before a storm."

"I wish Papa would come home," said Sadie. A big tear glistened on her red cheek.

"He'll be home as soon as he can," Charlie told her. "He is needed in Lawrence."

"I only wish we'd hear more news," said Ida Jane.

Flory bit her lip and for once was silent. *Flory is worried about her father too,* Charlie realized.

Just then Ida Jane pointed. "Look, there's Mr. Engle's horse. Maybe he knows something."

"The free-state men in Lawrence are busy building forts and preparing for an attack," Mr. Engle was telling

Momma as they burst in. "But supplies are short. Wagons loaded with apples, potatoes, and flour have been stopped at the border ruffians' camp near the Wakarusa River, a few miles from town."

Charlie remembered the wagon he had seen in town, loaded with goods from Missouri. If the wagons stopped coming, where would their food come from?

Mr. Engle looked at Momma. "Be careful with your supplies. Try to make your food last. I know James will be back as soon as he can."

"We must do our part to make Kansas free," said Momma. "Still, I never dreamed it would be this hard."

Flory was right about the sky. On Saturday afternoon the temperature dropped. The wind began to blow in great gusts. It whistled through the cabin like a teakettle.

Charlie and Ida Jane cut more prairie grass to pack inside the crude stable Papa had built. They made sure the oxen and Annie and her calf had water to drink.

"We'll have to come back later and break through the ice on top of the water bucket," said Ida Jane. "Otherwise they won't be able to drink."

"Let's pack extra grass in your chicken boxes to

keep them warm," Flory suggested to Sadie.

The chickens were Sadie's favorites. She was especially proud that she and Lion had managed to keep five little chicks safe all summer and fall.

"No coyotes are going to get our chickens!" Sadie liked to say, wrapping her arms around the dog's neck.

All afternoon the children dragged more wood inside and piled it in a corner of the cabin. By midafternoon snow and sleet had begun to beat against the cabin roof.

It was almost dark when Flory slapped her hand against her forehead. "I almost forgot the most important thing!"

"What's that?" asked Charlie.

"Charlie, does your daddy keep a long rope in his stable?" Flory asked.

"Yes, but what do we need with rope?"

"It could snow for days," explained Flory. "And we still need to tend to the animals. Last year in Missouri we heard stories of folks out here on the prairie getting lost trying to find their own barns in blizzards."

"Our animals aren't very far away," argued Ida Jane.

"But it's easy to get lost in a big snowstorm. That's

why you need a rope strung between the house and the stable."

Charlie gulped. It was so cold all he wanted to do was crawl under the quilts and sleep. *But I'm nine now*, he thought. *Papa is depending on me to help.*

"I can go," Charlie said.

"Good," said Flory. "Tie one end of the rope to the hitching post. Then tie the other around your waist and come back. Next time we have to check the animals, we can hold on to the rope to find our way."

Ida Jane was putting wood on the fire. "Don't forget to make it a good, tight knot, Charlie."

Charlie sighed. He felt like telling Ida Jane that since she knew so much, maybe she should go. But he didn't. He put his coat on, grabbed the lantern, and stepped outside.

Into a blizzard.

CHAPTER
ELEVEN

"Ouch!"

Charlie put his hands up to cover his face. The wind was blowing sideways, right at him. Sharp pricks of ice cut his skin.

Charlie made his eyes as small as he could to keep the icy pellets out. Squinting, he stopped to look around. *I have to get my bearings,* he reminded himself. *I need to know exactly where everything is.*

To his right was the place where Momma had made her kitchen garden last summer. To his left was his favorite hill, where he could see the fields stretching away to the creek.

The stable was straight ahead. Charlie trudged toward it slowly, head down.

One step at a time, he told himself.

One, two, three, four . . . Charlie counted to sixty. At

last he reached the stable. He made sure the animals had grain and hay. He cut through the thin layer of ice on the top of the water troughs with a hatchet.

Next Charlie found some rope.

"I hope it's long enough," he said out loud. Annie, the cow, gazed at him, chewing slowly. Momma had bought Annie from a woman whose husband and child had died of fever. The woman had decided to leave Kansas.

Charlie wondered if his own family would leave Kansas. Would they stay if something bad happened to Papa? Or would Momma decide that life here was too hard and want to go home?

Charlie tied two lengths of rope together and slipped the handle of the lantern over his arm. "All right," he told Annie. "Now I can go back."

The door almost flew off in his hand. The wind was just as fierce as before. Charlie felt as if he were being hit with hundreds of glass slivers.

Shivering hard, he stopped to tie one end of the rope to the hitching post. He used the knots Papa had taught him. Then he turned toward the cabin. He could barely see it in the swirling snow.

Think, he told himself. *Move carefully.*

Charlie clutched the lantern in one hand and the rope in the other. He took one step, then another.

Suddenly he remembered that Flory had warned him to tie the rope around his waist so he wouldn't drop it.

It was hard to do, and he had to put the lantern down between his boots. But at last Charlie got the rope tied around his waist.

As he bent to pick up the lantern again, something made him turn around. He wasn't sure just what. Maybe it was a sound or maybe just a feeling.

A feeling that someone was out there.

CHAPTER

TWELVE

Charlie squinted and stared into the growing darkness. He tried to make out shapes in the driving snow.

Is that a horse on the path we take to the road? he asked himself. *It almost looks like one.*

The wind paused for just a second, as though trying to catch its breath. In that instant Charlie thought he heard a familiar high-pitched sound. Almost like a whistle.

A whistle! Charlie stared at the shape again. Yes, it was definitely a horse. And next to it was a smaller shape that seemed to be waving at him.

Why, it was Mr. Morgan!

Why isn't Mr. Morgan riding? Charlie wondered. Was he hurt?

Mr. Morgan was farther away than the cabin, but Charlie had made his length of rope extra-long. Maybe it would reach.

I must go help him, Charlie told himself.

Charlie felt scared as he walked away from the cabin. But he kept going, one step at a time. The rope stayed around his waist. Would it reach? Yes!

At last he got close enough to see that Mr. Morgan and his horse both were limping toward him slowly.

"Charlie!" yelled Mr. Morgan. He threw his arm over Charlie's shoulder. "Thank goodness I spotted your lantern. I've come back for Flory. But I was afraid I'd miss your cabin in this storm."

Mr. Morgan leaned on Charlie as they slowly made their way back to the stable. Charlie pulled the door open, and Mr. Morgan sank to the ground, clutching his ankle.

"I'll take care of your horse," said Charlie. "What happened?"

"The wind spooked him. He tripped in a hole and threw me off. I believe he'll be all right, but I didn't dare ride him. I think my ankle is worse than his."

Charlie unsaddled Mr. Morgan's horse and gave him some hay and water. "We'd better get back to the cabin."

Mr. Morgan got up. "Let me lean on your shoulder, Charlie."

Just then the door flew open. A man stood in the doorway. "Get away from my boy!"

"Papa!"

At first Charlie was afraid Papa had a gun. Then he realized Papa was holding a wooden rocking chair above his head. He was about to crack Flory's dad over the head with it.

"Papa, it's all right!" Charlie yelled. He ran to give Papa a hug. Papa set the chair down and put his arm around Charlie.

"What's going on here, Charlie?" Papa asked, frowning. "Who is this?"

"This is Flory's father," said Charlie. "Flory is my friend from the steamboat. She's staying with us."

Flory's father stuck out his hand. "I'm Jake Morgan. I'm from Missouri, and I live in Franklin. But I'm not a violent man, and I mean your family no harm. With the latest trouble I feared for my daughter's safety. Your wife was kind enough to let her stay here until the trouble blew over."

Papa still frowned. "Are Momma and the girls all right, Charlie?"

Mr. Morgan and Charlie looked at each other.

Then Charlie smiled. "You brought this chair just in time, Papa."

CHAPTER
THIRTEEN

Charlie thought the small cabin had never seemed so cozy. The storm raged outside, but inside, seven people, one new baby, and one excited dog made so much noise no one seemed to notice the fierce prairie winds.

"The trouble is over for now, and Lawrence is safe from attack," Papa told them, warming his hands by the fire. "Sheriff Jones and his men should be heading back to Missouri tomorrow."

"I hope the peace treaty Governor Shannon signed will last," said Mr. Morgan with a sigh. "I settled in Franklin to be near folks from back home. But I don't hold with trying to settle the future of Kansas with violence."

"I'm afraid we haven't seen the end of violence in Kansas," replied Papa. "Once the winter is over, I think we're in for more trouble.

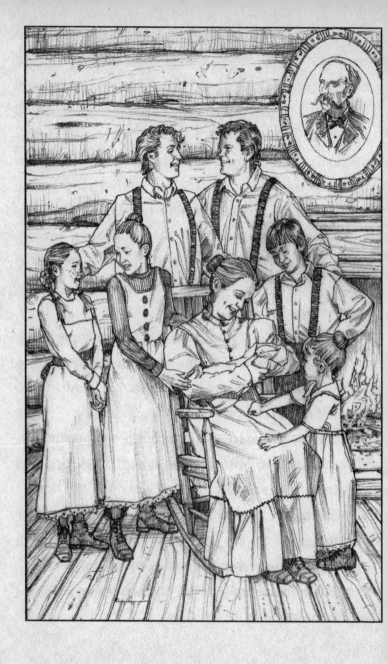

"Oh, but I'm almost forgetting my good news," Papa went on. "We got a letter from Grandpa. Everyone at home is fine, even our old dog, Danny. Grandpa and Uncle John sent some money to help us buy extra food this winter."

"So that's how you had enough to buy this wonderful chair," said Momma, rocking Baby Henry by the fire. "Still, I can't help wondering. Is fighting to make Kansas a free state worth this hardship? Families can't spare their menfolk during these harsh, cold times. Thank goodness I had my children to help these last two weeks."

Sadie piped up. "I did the dishes *every* night, Papa. And I helped Ida Jane make apple cake. I put the spices in."

Ida Jane hesitated, then smiled at Flory. "Flory helped too. She helped us get ready for the blizzard."

"And she sang us a beautiful song," added Momma with a smile.

"Wait!" yelled Flory. "We're forgetting Charlie!"

"That's right," said Papa. "Charlie was brave enough to drive the wagon home from Lawrence alone."

"And he ran to get Mrs. Engle when Momma needed help," said Ida Jane.

"Charlie went to the stable in the storm," put in Sadie.

"And don't forget, Charlie helped me get here safely with my hurt ankle," said Mr. Morgan.

Lion barked once and sat down beside Charlie. Charlie blushed and buried his head in his dog's fur.

Charlie didn't know if the troubles in Kansas were over or what would happen next spring. He wasn't even sure his family would make it to spring. But right now, in their little cabin in the snow, Charlie felt happy.

"I have an idea," said Charlie softly. "Since Papa wasn't here for our day of thanksgiving, maybe we could celebrate tomorrow. Maybe we could even bake a pie with the apples Flory brought us."

Flory clapped her hands. "That would be tremendously wonderful!"

❋APPLE FRUIT CAKE❋

Author's note: This recipe was recorded by Alice Kirk Grierson (1828–1888) and adapted for modern use by volunteers of the National Park Service Southwest Region. When I made it, I chopped the apples after they were tender. It baked for two hours, filling the house with the smell of molasses and spices. It makes a rich, large, spicy cake, with an old-fashioned taste like gingerbread. If you like molasses, you will think it tastes "tremendously wonderful."

MRS. GRIERSON'S ORIGINAL RECIPE

2 cups dried apples soaked over night,
chopped fine, and cooked in 2 cups of molasses.
When cold add 2 cups sugar, 1 cup butter,
5 cups flour, 3 eggs, 1 cup milk, 1 teaspoonful
soda, spice of all kinds.

MODERN VERSION

We changed the procedure but did not alter the ingredients except to designate amounts of the various spices we used.

Cover dried apples with cold water. Place over
heat, and simmer for 30 minutes, or until the
apples are tender. Drain well and set aside.
Sift the flour with the baking soda and add:

2 teaspoons cinnamon
2 teaspoons nutmeg
1 teaspoon mace
2 teaspoons allspice
1 teaspoon ground cloves

Set aside the sifted ingredients.
Cream the butter and sugar until light.
Add the eggs, one at a time, and beat well.
Add the sifted dry ingredients to the creamed mix-
ture alternately with the milk. Blend
in the apples and the molasses.

Turn the batter into a greased 10-inch tube
pan or Bundt pan, and bake in a 300-degree oven
for about 2 hours, or until the cake tests done.

SHENANDOAH

"Shenandoah" is one of America's best-loved folk songs. It is a traditional river shanty, or work song, sung by sailors on the Missouri and Mississippi rivers. Most people think the song tells the tale of a white trader who falls in love with the daughter of an Algonquin chief named Shenandoah. There are many different versions and variations of this beautiful song.

Oh, Shenandoah, I long to hear you,
Way hey, you rolling river!
Oh, Shenandoah, I long to hear you.
Away, we're bound away
'cross the wide Missouri.

Oh, Shenandoah, I love your daughter,
Way hey, you rolling river!
Oh, Shenandoah, I love your daughter.
Away, we're bound away
'cross the wide Missouri.

Missouri she's a mighty river,
Way hey, you rolling river!
When she rolls down, her topsails shiver.
Away, we're bound away
'cross the wide Missouri.

For seven years I courted Sally,
Way hey, you rolling river!
For seven more, I longed to have her.
Away, we're bound away
'cross the wide Missouri.

Farewell, my dear, I'm bound to leave you,
Way hey, you rolling river!
Oh, Shenandoah, I'll not deceive you.
Away, we're bound away
'cross the wide Missouri.

ABOUT
CABIN IN THE SNOW

Although parts of this story are based on historical events, Charlie and his family and friends are fictional characters. *Cabin in the Snow* takes place at a time when people were debating if slavery should spread to America's territories in the West. There were many tensions between the North and the South at this time too.

The Kansas-Nebraska Act of 1854 created the territories of Kansas and Nebraska. It ended the Missouri Compromise, an agreement in 1820 that forbade slavery in the lands of the Louisiana Purchase except for Missouri, and it changed the law about whether slavery could spread to the territories by stating that Kansas would be a free state or a slave state on the basis of how the people in Kansas voted.

The act began to cause problems almost immediately. Free-soil northerners and people from proslavery Missouri flocked to Kansas to have a voice in the territory's future. Since the groups wanted different things, they soon clashed.

The events of the fall of 1855 are known as the Wakarusa War (the Wakarusa is a river near Lawrence). The trouble began on November 21, 1855, when a free-soil settler named Charles Dow was shot by his neighbor, Franklin Coleman, a proslavery man. A few days later Sheriff Samuel Jones (who had been appointed by proslavery legislators) arrested Mr. Dow's friend Jacob Branson. After Branson was rescued by his friends, Sheriff Jones threatened to attack Lawrence. Luckily the attack was avoided, and on December 8 a peace agreement was signed.

Besides Charles Dow, one other person died in the Wakarusa War. His name was Thomas W. Barber. Like Charlie's father, Barber had gone to Lawrence to help defend the town. He was shot on December 6, 1855, on his way home to visit his wife in their cabin several miles from Lawrence.

Unfortunately the peace between the two sides did not last. More trouble lay ahead in the spring and summer of 1856. You can find out what happened in *Our Kansas Home*, the third book in the Prairie Skies series. For more information about Kansas history, visit the Kansas State Historical Society Web site at www.kshs.org.